For Paul,
without whom I'd never
write a word! Thanks
for all your help.

B—

8-29-44
state College

BOOKS BY BRUCE WEIGL

POETRY

Song of Napalm
The Monkey Wars
A Romance
The Executioner
A Sack Full of Old Quarrels

CRITICISM

The Imagination As Glory: On the Poetry of
    James Dickey (coeditor, with T. R. Hummer)
The Giver of Morning: On Dave Smith (editor)

# SONG OF NAPALM

The Atlantic Monthly Press
New York

# SONG

# OF

# NAPALM

P
O
E
M
S   by

Bruce

Weigl

Published simultaneously in Canada

Printed in the United States of America

Library of Congress Cataloging-in-Publication Data

Weigl, Bruce, 1949-
  Song of napalm.

  1. Vietnamese Conflict, 1961-1975—Poetry.
I. Title.
PS3573.E3835S65 1988      811'.54      88-6161
ISBN 0-87113-241-9

Design by Julie Duquet

The Atlantic Monthly Press
19 Union Square West
New York, NY 10003

First printing

# ACKNOWLEDGMENTS

Grateful acknowledgment is made to the following publications in which many of these poems first appeared: *Back Door, The Black Warrior Review, Field, Ironwood, Mother Jones, The Missouri Review, The New England Review, Open Places, Quarterly West, Tendril,* and *Tar River Poetry.*

"The Last Lie" appeared originally in *Poetry Now.*

"Sailing to Bien Hoa" appeared originally in *Western Humanities Review.*

"Song of Napalm," "Amnesia," "Snowy Egret," "The Kiss," "Apparition of the Exile," and "Breakdown" appeared originally in *TriQuarterly,* a publication of Northwestern University.

"The Way of Tet" and "On the Anniversary of Her Grace" appeared originally in *Prairie Schooner,* and appears by permission of University of Nebraska Press. Copyright © 1988 by the University of Nebraska Press.

"Monkey," "Mines," "Hand to Hand," "The Sharing," "Dogs," "Him, on the Bicycle," "When Saigon Was French," "Convoy," "Sailing to Bien Hoa," "Short," "A Romance," and "Anna Grasa" appeared in *A Romance* (The University of Pittsburgh

Press, 1979); "Amnesia," "Surrounding Blues on the Way Down," "Temple Near Quang Tri, Not on the Map," "The Last Lie," "Burning Shit at An Khe," "Song for the Lost Private," "Girl at the Chu Lai Laundry," "Mercy," "Snowy Egret," and "Song of Napalm" appeared in *The Monkey Wars* (The University of Georgia Press, 1984).

"Temple Near Quang Tri, Not on the Map" also appeared in *Pushcart V* (1980).

Additionally, many of these poems appeared in the following anthologies: *Carrying the Darkness: American Indochina—The Poetry of the Vietnam War*; *New American Poets of the 80's*; *Reading the Wind: Literature of the Vietnam War*; *The Morrow Anthology of Younger American Poets*; *The Writer in Our World* (Atlantic Monthly Press); *Unwinding the Vietnam War*; *Vietnam Anthology: American War Literature*; *Vietnam Reconsidered: Lessons from a War*.

The author would also like to thank the following people for their special assistance and support: Gloria Emerson, Stuart Friebert, Ann Godoff, Larry Moffi, Phil Raisor, Charles Simic, Dave Smith, Alberta Turner, James Wright, David Young, and Paul Zimmer.

*For Miss Tao of the tiger cage*

"My home, my country,
the heart split in two . . ."

*And for Reg Gibbons*

# TEMPLE NEAR QUANG TRI, NOT ON THE MAP


Dusk, the ivy thick with sparrows
squawking for more room
is all we hear; we see
birds move on the walls of the temple
shaping their calligraphy of wings.
Ivy is thick in the grottoes,
on the moon-watching platform
and ivy keeps the door from fully closing.

The point man leads us and we are
inside, lifting
the white washbowl, the smaller bowl
for rice, the stone lanterns
and carved stone heads that open
above the carved faces for incense.
But even the bamboo sleeping mat
rolled in the corner,
even the place of prayer, is clean.
And a small man

sits legs askew in the shadow
the farthest wall casts

halfway across the room.
He is bent over, his head
rests on the floor and he is speaking something
as though to us and not to us.
The CO wants to ignore him;
he locks and loads and fires a clip into the walls
which are not packed with rice this time
and tells us to move out.

But one of us moves towards the man,
curious about what he is saying.
We bend him to sit straight
and when he's nearly peaked
at the top of his slow uncurling
his face becomes visible, his eyes
roll down to the charge
wired between his teeth and the floor.
The sparrows
burst off the walls into the jungle.

# HIM, ON THE BICYCLE

*"There was no light; there was no light at all . . ."*
———*Roethke*

In a liftship near Hue,
the door gunner is in a trance.
He's that driver who falls
asleep at the wheel
between Pittsburgh and Cleveland
staring at the Ho Chi Minh Trail.

Flares fall,
where the river leaps
I go stiff,
I have to think, tropical.

The door gunner sees movement,
the pilot makes small circles:
four men running, carrying rifles,
one man on a bicycle.

He pulls me out of the ship,
there's firing far away.
I'm on the back of the bike

holding his hips.
It's hard pumping for two,
I hop off and push the bike.

I'm brushing past trees,
the man on the bike stops pumping,
lifts his feet,
we don't waste a stroke.
His hat flies off,
I catch it behind my back,
put it on, I want to live forever!

Like a blaze
streaming down the trail.

## SOME THOUGHTS ON THE
## AMBASSADOR: BONG SON, 1967

Bunker the ambassador.

Does Mr. Bunker have a bunker?

He must have a bunker
with chrome faucets and a sauna
and a mama san to ease his mind.

They must call it
Mr. Bunker's bunker.

He must be shaking his head.

# HAND TO HAND

We sit in a circle around First Sergeant. Who wants to try me he says and my hand goes up and before I know what I'm doing I'm doing it. He slams me into the ground like someone made of water—my back, my lungs, some clouds. I take his hand and he spins me and I'm down again. I can feel the day lost, the night I'm in my rack, hurt, unable to sleep, he comes like so much man, leads me past the fireguard, past fifty sleeping soldiers, pushes his bunk aside, pulls me and we dance and I learn hand to hand brothers, learn the places on the body that betray. . . . Close my eyes. Open them. Fall violently upward.

# SURROUNDING BLUES
# ON THE WAY DOWN


I was barely in country.
We slipped under the rain-black clouds
opening around us like orchids.
He'd come to take me into the jungle
so I felt the loneliness
though I did not yet hate the beautiful war.
Eighteen years old and a man
was telling me how to stay alive
in the tropics he said would rot me—

brothers of the heart he said and smiled
until we came upon a mama san
bent over from her stuffed sack of flowers.
We flew past her but he hit the brakes hard,
he spun the tires backwards in the mud.
He did not hate the war either
but other reasons made him cry out to her
so she stopped,
she smiled her beetle-black teeth at us,
in the air she raised her arms.

I have no excuse for myself.
I sat in that man's jeep in the rain

and watched him slam her to her knees,
the plastic butt of his M16
crashing down on her.
I was barely in country, the clouds
hung like huge flowers, black
like her teeth.

# SONG FOR THE LOST PRIVATE

The night we were to meet in the hotel
in the forbidden Cholon district
you didn't show
so I drank myself into a filthy room with a bar girl
who had terrible scars
she ran her fingers over
as we bartered for the night.
Drunk, I couldn't do anything, angry
I threw the mattress to the street
and stood naked on the balcony
cursing your name to the night.
She thought I was crazy
and tried to give my money back.
I don't know how to say I tried again.
I saw myself in the mirror and couldn't move.
In her fist she crushed the paper money,
she curled in sleep away from me
so I felt cruel, cold, and small arms fire
cracked in the marketplace below.
I thought I heard you call back my name then
but white flares lit the sky
casting empty streets in clean light

and the firing stopped.
I couldn't sleep so I touched her
small shoulders, traced the curve on her spine,
traced the scars, the miles
we were all from home.

# SHORT

There's a bar girl on Trung Hung Do who has half a ten-piaster note I tore in my drunken relief to be leaving the country. She has half and I have half, if I can find it. If I lost it, it wasn't on purpose, it's all I have to remember her. She has a wet sheet, a PX fan, PX radio, and half a ten-piaster note, as if she cared to remember me. She thought it was stupid to tear money and when I handed it to her she turned to another soldier, new in country, who needed a girl. I hope I burn in hell.

# THE LAST LIE

Some guy in the miserable convoy
raised up in the back of our open truck
and threw a can of C rations at a child
who called into the rumble for food.
He didn't toss the can, he wound up and hung it
on the child's forehead and she was stunned
backwards into the dust of our trucks.

Across the sudden angle of the road's curving
I could still see her when she rose,
waving one hand across her swollen, bleeding head,
wildly swinging her other hand
at the children who mobbed her,
who tried to take her food.

I grit my teeth to myself to remember that girl
smiling as she fought off her brothers and sisters.
She laughed

as if she thought it were a joke
and the guy with me laughed
and fingered the edge of another can
like it was the seam of a baseball
until his rage ripped
again into the faces of children
who called to us for food.

# MONKEY

1

I am you are he she it is
we are you are they are.
I am you are he she it is
we are you are they are.
When they ask for your number
pretend to be breathing.
Forget the stinking jungle,
force your fingers between the lines.
Learn to get out of the dew.
The snakes are thirsty.
Bladders, water, boil it, drink it.
Get out of your clothes.
You can't move in your green clothes.
Your O.D. in color issues clothes.
Get out the plates and those who ate,
those who spent the night.
Those small Vietnamese soldiers.
They love to hold your hand.

Back away from their dark cheeks.
Small Vietnamese soldiers.
They love to love you.
I have no idea how it happened.
I remember nothing but light.

2

I don't remember the hard
swallow of the lover.
I don't remember the burial of ears.
I don't remember
the time of the explosion.
This is the place where curses are manufactured,
delivered like white tablets.
The survivor is spilling his bedpan.
He slips a curse into your pocket,
you're finally satisfied.
I don't remember the heat
in the hands,
the heat around the neck.

Good times bad times sleep
get up work. Sleep get up
good times bad times.

Work eat sleep good bad work times.
I like a certain cartoon of wounds.
The water which refused to dry.
I like a little unaccustomed mercy.
Pulling the trigger is all we have.
I hear a child.

3

I dropped to the bottom of a well.
I have a knife.
I cut someone with it.
Oh, I have the petrified eyebrows
of my Vietnam monkey.
My monkey from Vietnam.
My monkey.
Put your hand here.
It makes no sense.
I beat the monkey.
I didn't know him.
He was bloody.
He lowered his intestines
to my shoes. My shoes
spit-shined the moment
I learned to tie the bow.
I'm not on speaking terms

with anyone. In the wrong climate
a person can spoil,
the way a pair of boots slows you. . . .

I don't know when I'm sleeping.
I don't know if what I'm saying
is anything at all.
I'll lie on my monkey bones.

4

I'm tired of the rice
falling in slow motion
like eggs from the smallest animal.
I'm twenty-five years old,
quiet, tired of the same mistakes,
the same greed, the same past.
The same past with its bleat
and pound of the dead,
with its hand grenade
tossed into a hooch on a dull Sunday
because when a man dies like that
his eyes sparkle,
his nose fills with witless nuance
because a farmer in Bong Son
has dead cows lolling
in a field of claymores
because the VC tie hooks to their comrades
because a spot of blood is a number

because a woman is lifting
her dress across the big pond.

If we're soldiers we should smoke them
if we have them. Someone's bound
to point us in the right direction
sooner or later.

I'm tired and I'm glad you asked.

5

There is a hill.
Men run top hill.
Men take hill.
Give hill to man.

Me and my monkey
and me and my monkey
my Vietnamese monkey
my little brown monkey
came with me
to Guam and Hawaii
in Ohio he saw
all my people he
jumped on my daddy
he slipped into mother
he baptized my sister
he's my little brown monkey
he came here from heaven

to give me his spirit
imagine my monkey my beautiful
monkey he saved me lifted
me above the punji
sticks above the mines
above the ground burning
above the dead above
the living above the
wounded dying the wounded
dying.

# II

## SONG OF NAPALM

"The abnormal is not courage . . ."
                                    Jack Gilbert

# SONG OF NAPALM

*for my wife*

After the storm, after the rain stopped pounding,
we stood in the doorway watching horses
walk off lazily across the pasture's hill.
We stared through the black screen,
our vision altered by the distance
so I thought I saw a mist
kicked up around their hooves when they faded
like cut-out horses
away from us.
The grass was never more blue in that light, more
scarlet; beyond the pasture
trees scraped their voices into the wind, branches
crisscrossed the sky like barbed wire
but you said they were only branches.

Okay. The storm stopped pounding.
I am trying to say this straight: for once
I was sane enough to pause and breathe
outside my wild plans and after the hard rain

I turned my back on the old curses. I believed
they swung finally away from me . . .

But still the branches are wire
and thunder is the pounding mortar,
still I close my eyes and see the girl
running from her village, napalm
stuck to her dress like jelly,
her hands reaching for the no one
who waits in waves of heat before her.

So I can keep on living,
so I can stay here beside you,
I try to imagine she runs down the road and wings
beat inside her until she rises
above the stinking jungle and her pain
eases, and your pain, and mine.

But the lie swings back again.
The lie works only as long as it takes to speak
and the girl runs only as far
as the napalm allows

until her burning tendons and crackling
muscles draw her up
into that final position
burning bodies so perfectly assume. Nothing
can change that, she is burned behind my eyes
and not your good love and not the rain-swept air
and not the jungle-green
pasture unfolding before us can deny it.

# BURNING SHIT AT AN KHE

Into that pit
   I had to climb down
with a rake and matches; eventually,
   you had to do something
because it just kept piling up
   and it wasn't our country, it wasn't
our air thick with the sick smoke
   so another soldier and I
lifted the shelter off its blocks
   to expose the homemade toilets:
fifty-five-gallon drums cut in half
   with crude wood seats that splintered.
We soaked the piles in fuel oil
   and lit the stuff
and tried to keep the fire burning.
   To take my first turn
I paid some kid
   a CARE package of booze from home.
I'd walked past the burning once
   and gagged the whole heart of myself—
it smelled like the world
   was on fire,
but when my turn came again
   there was no one

so I stuffed cotton up my nose
    and marched up that hill. We poured
and poured until it burned and black
    smoke curdled
but the fire went out.
    Heavy artillery
hammered the evening away in the distance,
    Vietnamese laundry women watched
from a safe place, laughing.
    I'd grunted out eight months
of jungle and thought I had a grip on things
    but we flipped the coin and I lost
and climbed down into my fellow soldiers'
    shit and began to sink and didn't stop
until I was deep to my knees. Liftships
    cut the air above me, the hacking
blast of their blades
    ripped dust in swirls so every time
I tried to light a match
    it died
and it all came down on me, the stink
    and the heat and the worthlessness
until I slipped and climbed
    out of that hole and ran

past the olive-drab
   tents and trucks and clothes and everything
green as far from the shit
   as the fading light allowed.
Only now I can't fly.
   I lay down in it
and fingerpaint the words of who I am
   across my chest
until I'm covered and there's only one smell,
   one word.

# CONVOY

On a convoy from Bong Son to Hue we stop at a Vietnamese graveyard. People set up shelter halves right over the top of gravestones: one rock wall just in case. It's raining. I smell people.

Two in the morning someone wakes me for guard. I'm out of bed, standing in the cold. The man next to me walks over to talk. A helicopter is parked thirty yards in front of us and in the moon it begins to move. My friend becomes leader, he wants to fire, I'm afraid of an explosion. He tells me to circle the ship while he covers.

At the window it's dark, no moon. Inside, the pilot, restlessly turning in his sleep, rocking his ship.

## LZ NOWHERE

Nights I spent on the dusty runway
under the green liftship

tethered down from the wind of the highlands
shaping the moonlit fields

surrounding us like care.
I stroked the length of the blades

those nights
and moved the rudder and flaps

so it felt like legs parting
or someone's arms opening to me.

## DOGS

I bought a bar girl in Saigon
cigarettes, watches, and Tide soap
to sell on the black market
and she gave me a room to sleep in
and all the cocaine I could live through
those nights when I had to leave.
I would sometimes meet them on the stairs,
and she would be wrapped in the soldier
who was always drunk, smiling,
her smell all over him.

She ran once to the room screaming
about dogs and pulled me down to the street
where a crowd of Vietnamese gathered
watching two stuck.
The owners fought about whose fault it was.
The owner of the male took off his sandal,
began to beat the female;
the owner of the female
kicked the male
but they did not part.
The beating made her tighten

41

and her tightening made him swell
and she dragged him down the street
the crowd running after them.

I remembered my grandfather,
how his pit bull locked up
the same way with the neighbor's dog.
The neighbor screamed and kicked
and the cop with the nightstick
sucked his teeth and circled
the dogs as the dogs circled.
Yet my grandfather knew what to do—
not cold water, warm,
warm and pour it slow.

# MINES

### 1

In Vietnam I was always afraid of mines:
North Vietnamese mines, Vietcong mines,
French mines, American mines,
whole fields marked with warning signs.

A Bouncing Betty comes up waist-high—
cuts you in half.
One man's legs were laid
alongside him in the dust-off,
he asked for a chairback, morphine,
he screamed he wanted to give
his eyes away, his kidneys,
his heart. . . .

### 2

Here is how you walk at night: slowly lift
one leg, clear the sides with your arms, clear the back,
front, put the leg down, like swimming.

## WHEN SAIGON WAS FRENCH

I remember Françoise crossing
the room in a naked blur
in the hotel on Trung Hung Do—
dark except for flares
falling into the cemetery
catching on the window
as if the caches of weapons would be visible.
She was looking for something, a cigarette
or some more clothes as it was her idiosyncrasy
to move around afterwards
as it was mine to lie still
with the understanding that this was a war
in which no one was called to duty,
a war with no fronts.
I was a day away from leaving
and didn't want to go—a boy
come ten thousand miles from Ohio
to fall in with a French girl,
to lord over my block of the black market
and spend my money on cocaine,
all that beautiful dying
when Saigon was French.

## MERCY

Enough snow over last night's ice
so the road appears safe, appears
as a long white scar unfolding.
Ohio, cold hawk off Lake Erie,
and only enough light to see vague outlines:
the castlelike shape of mill stacks
and the shape of gulls' wings
dipping to the parking lot for garbage
lashed this way and that by the wind
these nights have in common.
I pumped gasoline from five to midnight
for minimum wage
because I had a family and the war
made me stupid, and only dead enough
to clean windshields.
When you clean the windshields of others
you see your own face
reflected in the glass.
I looked and saw only enough hope
to lift me car to car and in between
I breathed the oil smell and the fly strips
and the vending-candy air.
The Gulf sign clanged in the gale,
the plate glass strained like a voice

I thought would shatter
but still cars came, dim headlights
casting the snow into a silver sheet,
then the fenders like low clouds,
then the bundled families
and the hushed sound
when father opened the window
and slipped me the money for gas.
Only a second when our eyes catch
and the wind shows some mercy.

# BREAKDOWN

With sleep that is barely under the surface
it begins, a twisting sleep as if a wire
were inside you and tried at night
to straighten your body.
Or it's like a twitch
through your nerves as you sleep
so you tear the sheet from the bed
to try to stop the pounding spine.
A lousy, worthless
sleep of strangers with guns,
children trapped in the alley,
the teenage soldiers glancing back
over their soldiers
the moment before
they squeeze the trigger.

I am going to stay here as long as I can.
I am going to sit in the garden as if nothing has happened
and let the bruised azaleas have their way.

# SNOWY EGRET

My neighbor's boy has lifted his father's shotgun and stolen
down to the backwaters of the Elizabeth
and in the moon he's blasted a snowy egret
from the shallows it stalked for small fish.

Midnight. My wife wakes me. He's in the backyard
with a shovel so I go down half drunk with pills
that let me sleep to see what I can see and if it's safe.
The boy doesn't hear me come across the dewy grass.
He says through tears he has to bury it,
he says his father will kill him
and he digs until the hole is deep enough and gathers
the egret carefully into his arms
as if not to harm the blood-splattered wings
gleaming in the flashlight beam.

His man's muscled shoulders
shake with the weight of what he can't set right no matter
    what,
but one last time he tries to stay a child, sobbing
please don't tell. . . .
He says he only meant to flush it from the shadows,
he only meant to watch it fly
but the shot spread too far

ripping into the white wings
spanned awkwardly for a moment
until it glided into brackish death.

I want to grab his shoulders,
Shake the lies loose from his lips but he hurts enough,
he burns with shame for what he's done,
with fear for his hard father's
fists I've seen crash down on him for so much less.
I don't know what to do but hold him.
If I let go he'll fly to pieces before me.
What a time we share, that can make a good boy steal away,
wiping out from the blue face of the pond
what he hadn't even known he loved, blasting
such beauty into nothing.

# III

## THE KISS

"What did I know, what did I know
of love's austere and lonely offices?"
—Robert Hayden

# AMNESIA

If there was a world more disturbing than this
where black clouds bowed down and swallowed you whole
and overgrown tropical plants
rotted, effervescent in the muggy twilight and monkeys
screamed something
that came to sound like words to each other
across the triple-canopy jungle you shared,
you don't remember it.

You tell yourself no and cry a thousand days.
You imagine the crows calling autumn into place
are your brothers and you could
if only the strength and will were there
fly up to them to be black
and useful to the wind.

## ON THE ANNIVERSARY
## OF HER GRACE

Rain and low clouds blown through the valley,
rain down the coast raising the brackish
rivers at their high tides too high,
rain and black skies that come for you.

Not excellent and fair,
I wake from a restless night of dreams of her
whom I will never have again
as surely as each minute passing
makes impossible another small fulfillment
until there's only a lingering
I remember, a kiss I had imagined
would come again and again to my face.

Inside me the war had eaten a hole.
I could not touch anyone.
The wind blew through me to the green place
where they still fell in their blood.
I could hear their voices at night.

I could not undress in the light
her body cast in the dark rented room.

I could keep the dragons at the gate.
I could paint my face and hide
as shadow in the triple-canopy jungle.
I could not eat or sleep then walk all day
and all night watch a moonlit path for movement.

I could draw leeches from my skin
with the tip of a lit cigarette
and dig a hole deep enough to save me
before the sun bloodied the hills we could not take
even with our lives
but I could not open my arms to her
that first night of forgiveness.
I could not touch anyone.
I thought my body would catch fire.

## APPARITION OF THE EXILE

There was another life of cool summer mornings, the dogwood air
and the slag stink so gray like our monsoon which we loved for
the rain and cool wind until the rot came into us. And I remember
the boys we were the evening of our departure, our mothers
waving through the train's black pluming exhaust; they were not
proud in their tears of our leaving, so don't tell me to shut up about
the war or I might pull something from my head, from my head,
from my head that you wouldn't want to see and whoever the
people are might be offended.

From the green country you reconstruct in your brain, from the
rubble and stink of your occupation, there is no moving out. A
sweet boy who got drunk and brave on our long ride into the State
draws a maze every day on white paper, precisely in his room of
years as if you could walk into it. All day he draws and imagines
his platoon will return from the burning river where he sent them
sixteen years ago into fire. He can't stop seeing the line of trees
explode in white phosphorus blossoms and the liftship sent for
them spinning uncontrollably beyond hope into the Citadel wall.
Only his mother comes these days, drying the fruit in her apron
or singing the cup of hot tea into his fingers which, like barbed
wire, web the air.

## A ROMANCE

The skinny red-haired girl gets up
from the bar and dances
over to the jukebox
and punches the buttons as if
she were playing the piano—
below the white points of her pelvis
an enormous belt buckle
shaped like the head of a snake
with two red rhinestone eyes
which she polishes with the heels of her hands
making circles on her own fine thighs
and looking up
she catches me staring, my lust like a flag
waving at her across the room
as her big mean boyfriend
runs hillbilly after hillbilly off the table
in paycheck nine-ball games of pool.

It is always like this with me in bars,
wanting women I know
I'll have to get my face
punched bloody to love.
Or she could be alone,
and I could be dull enough from the liquor

to imagine my face interesting enough to take her
into conversation while I count my money
hoping to Jesus I have enough
to get us both romantic.
I can't sleep anyway so I go to bars
and tell my giant lies to women
who have heard them from me,
from the thousands of me
out on the town with our impossible strategies
for no good reasons but our selves,
who are holy.

# THE SHARING

I have not ridden a horse much,
two, maybe three times,
a broken gray mare my cousin called Ghost,
then only in the fall
through the flat pastures of Ohio,
that's not much.
But I watched two Chinese tanks
roll out of the jungle side by side,
their turret guns feeling before them
like a man walking through his dream,
their tracks slapping the bamboo like hooves.

I can't name the gaits of a horse
except the canter
and that rocks you to the withers,
but I saw those arms,
those guns and did not know for a moment
what they were, but knew they were not horses
as they pulled themselves deep
into the jungle
until there was only the dull rattle of their tracks
and a boy on a gray horse
flying through the opening fields.

# ON THE EVENING BEFORE
# HIS DEPARTURE

On the evening before his departure
he drove restlessly down back streets
as if there were a door
that had been there all along
and he could find it now and
slide through and escape to another life
where the stars would not explode
in his face. And then he drank
beer with friends
who did not dare say
the brutally simple good-byes
but drank hard with him and touched
each other in their drunkenness and

months later, lives later,
leeches and rot and words
like a ball of steel in his mouth,
he would lie with another boy in the razor grass,

his stomach torn open and
glistening in light breaking through
the canopies of green,
and he would remember them,
their grace undone,
then lose them forever in war's wind swirling
and give himself to the dying boy
who begged above the liftship blast
not to tell his mother.

## ANNA GRASA

I came home from Vietnam.
My father had a sign
made at the foundry:
WELCOME HOME BRUCE
in orange glow paint.
He rented spotlights,
I had to squint.
WELCOME HOME BRUCE.

Out of the car I moved
up on the sign
dreaming myself full,
the sign that cut the sky,
my eyes burned,

but behind the terrible thing
I saw my grandmother,

beautiful Anna Grasa.
I couldn't tell her.

I clapped to myself,
clapped to the sound of her dress.
I could have put it on
she held me so close.
Both of us could be inside.

# THE SOLDIER'S BRIEF EPISTLE

You think you're better than me,
cleaner or more good

because I did what you may have only
imagined as you leaned over the crib

or watched your woman sleep.
You think you're far away from me

but you're right here in my pants
and I can grab your throat

like a cock and squeeze.
And you want to know what it's like

before I go. It's like
a bad habit, pulling the trigger,

like a dream come true.
And he did not hide well enough

I would tell his family
in a language they do not understand,

but he did not cry out,
and he was very difficult to kill.

# DIALECTICAL MATERIALISM

Through dark tenements and fallen temples
we wander into Old Hanoi,
oil lamps glowing in small
storefronts and restaurants
where those, so long ago my enemy,
sit on low chairs and praise the simple evening.
On one block
the rich steam from pho,
their morning and evening soup, rises,
on another
brown smoked ducks are strung up in a row.
The people talk and smoke,
men hold each other's hands again in that old way
and children,
their black and white laughter all around us,
kick the weighted feather
with such grace into the air
because the bombs have stopped. And further

to the Long Bien bridge
where we meet a man
filling buckets
hung across his back's yoke
to bring cool water to his corn

in the moonlight.
When we ask our questions
he points to a stone and stick
house beyond the dikes
one thousand meters from the bridge
our great planes
could not finally knock down.
He doesn't say
how he must have huddled
those nights with his family,
how he must have spread himself
over them
until the village bell
called them back to their beds.
There are questions which
people who have everything
ask people who have nothing
and they do not understand.

*Hanoi, December 1985*

# THE KISS

All the good-byes said and done
I climbed into the plane and sat down.
From the cold I was shaking and ached
to be away from the love
of those waving through the frozen window . . .

(Once as a boy I was lost in a storm,
funnel cloud twisting so near
I was pitched from my bicycle
into the ditch,
picked up by the wind and yellow sky,
my arms before me
feeling my way through the wind
I could not cry above.
Out of that black air of debris,
out of nowhere, my father bent down,
lifted me and ran
to the house of strangers.)

And again that day on the plane
he appeared to me,

my forgotten orders in his hands.
He bent down to put the envelope into my lap,
on my lips he kissed me hard
and without a word he was gone
into the cold again.
Through the jungle, through the highlands,
through all that green dying
I touched my fingers to my lips.

# ELEGY

Into sunlight they marched,
into dog day, into no saints day,
and were cut down.
They marched without knowing
how the air would be sucked from their lungs,
how their lungs would collapse,
how the world would twist itself, would
bend into the cruel angles.

Into the black understanding they marched
until the angels came
calling their names,
until they rose, one by one from the blood.
The light blasted down on them.
The bullets sliced through the razor grass
so there was not even time to speak.
The words would not let themselves be spoken.
Some of them died.
Some of them were not allowed to.

BRUCE WEIGL was born in Lorain, Ohio. He is the author of four previous books of poetry, and the editor of two collections of essays on contemporary American poets. His poetry, essays, articles, and reviews have appeared in such magazines and journals as *The American Poetry Review, Mother Jones, The Nation, The Ohio Review, TriQuarterly,* and others. In addition, his poetry has been widely anthologized, most recently in *The Morrow Anthology of Younger American Poets.* For his work he has been awarded a Pushcart Prize, The Academy of American Poets Prize, a research grant from Old Dominion University, a Pennsylvania Arts Council Grant, The "Breadloaf Fellowship in Poetry," a YADDO Foundation Fellowship, an award for "Contributions to American Culture" from the Vietnam Veterans of America in 1987, and a grant from the National Endowment for the Arts for Creative Writing. Weigl, who has taught at the University of Arkansas and Old Dominion University, currently teaches in the Writing Program at Pennsylvania State University. From 1967 to 1968, Weigl served with the First Air Cavalry in Vietnam.